PLANET EARTH

ECOSYSTEMS

By Jim Pipe

D0416643

Essex County Council Libraries

Copyright © ticktock Entertainment Ltd 2008

First published in Great Britain in 2008 by ticktock Media Ltd,
2 Orchard Business Centre, North Farm Road, Tunbridge Wells, Kent, TN2 3XF

ticktock project editor: Ruth Owen
ticktock picture researcher: Ruth Owen and Lizzie Knowles
ticktock project designer: Emma Randall
With thanks to: Mark Sachner, Suzy Gazlay and Elizabeth Wiggans, Elaine Wilkinson and Matt Harding

ISBN 978 1 84696 517 3 pbk
ISBN 978 1 84696 689 7 hbk
Printed in China

A CIP catalogue record for this book is available from the British Library.

No part of this publication may be reproduced, copied, stored in a retrieval system or transmitted in any form or by any means electronic, mechanical, photocopying, recording or otherwise without prior written permission of the copyright owner.

Photography by Bruce Elliot and JL Allwork

Picture credits (t=top; b=bottom; c=centre; l=left; r=right):
Ingo Arndt/ Minden Pictures/ FLPA: 29tr. Jim Brandenburg/ Minden Pictures/ FLPA: 19bl. Nigel Cattlin/ FLPA: 17br.
Digital Stock: 9cbr. R. Dirscher/ FLPA: 22/23 main Gerry Ellis/ Minden Pictures/ FLPA: 6bl. Chris Fallows/ apexpredators.com:
14t. Michael & Patricia Fogden/ Minden Pitcures/ FLPA: 20tl. Michio Hoshino/ Minden Pictures/ FLPA: 10br. David Hosking/
FLPA: 21b, 27cr. iStock: 4/5. Thomas Lazar/ naturepl.com: 27tr. NASA/ ESA: 22tl. Fritz Polking: 25br. Michel Roggo/
naturepl.com: 11bl. Science Photo Library: 17bc. Shutterstock: OFC all,1all, 3, 4l, 4 inset x3, 5 inset x4, 6tl x4, 6/7 main, 7tl, 7cr
x2, 9tl, 9tr, 9 ctr, 9br, 9bl, 10t, 12 all, 13t, 14b all, 15 main, 15tr, 15cr, 16/17 main, 16tl, 16b x 3, 17cr, 17bl, 18, 19cl, 19tr, 19cr,
26t, 26c, 26b, 27tr, 27c, 27b, 28l x3, 28/29 main, 29br, 30 all, 31 all, OBC all. Jurgen & Christine Sohns/ FLPA: 8, 19br.
Superstock: 15br, 20 main, 22b, 23cr, 24bl, 25tr, 25cr, 26cl. Hayley Terry: 13b. Ticktock Media Archive: 11tl, 21t.
Konrad Wothe/ Minden Pictures/ FLPA: 24/25 main. Norbert Wu/ Minden Pictures/ FLPA: 23tr.

Every effort has been made to trace copyright holders, and we apologise in advance for any omissions.
We would be pleased to insert the appropriate acknowledgments in any subsequent edition of this publication.

CONTENTS

Your body is a small ecosystem. Inside you there are thousands of tiny organisms. These include the bacteria that help you digest your food!

A woodland is a large ecosystem with many plants and animals.

A single oak tree in the woodland can be an ecosystem all of its own.

In the oak tree there will be a community of birds, beetles, worms and fungi (above).

CHAPTER 1:
What Is An Ecosystem?

An ecosystem is a place and all the living things that live there and rely on each other to survive. Your home is a sort of ecosystem. You, your family, and pets depend on each other and the house itself to supply food, water, and shelter.

ECOSYSTEMS

An ecosystem supports a community, or group, of living things. The different plants and animals in an ecosystem depend on each other to survive. They also depend on nonliving things around them, such as the soil and water. Ecosystems can be enormous, like the Sahara Desert, or small, like a pond.

WHAT IS A HABITAT?

The word habitat refers just to the place where a plant or animal lives. For example, a fish and a mud worm may be part of the same river ecosystem. However, the fish's habitat is the water in the river, while the worm's habitat is the mud flat alongside the river.

WHAT IS A BIOME?

Scientists divide Earth into large areas called biomes. A biome is a region with the same climate and similar plants and animals. Each biome contains living things that are suited to the heat, soil, and water in that region. Each type of biome on our planet is found in many parts of the world. Within any one biome, there are many ecosystems made up of smaller communities of plants and animals.

EXAMPLES OF BIOMES

POLAR REGIONS
Polar regions make up one kind of biome. They are very cold, windy, and dry. Almost no plants can survive here. Animals such as polar bears, seals, and penguins get their food from the sea.

MOUNTAIN REGIONS
Mountain regions make up another biome. Mountains are cold, windy, and wet. Past a certain height, it is so cold that trees will not grow. This height is called the tree line.

DESERTS
Deserts make up a biome that is very hot and dry. Desert plants and animals need to survive with very little water. Desert temperatures are cooler at night. This is why desert animals are active at night.

Savannas are a type of biome found in South America and Africa. The African savanna is home to many kinds of wildlife and has many ecosystems. Here, a pride of lions watch a herd of zebra – their source of food. The lions and zebra are both members of the same ecosystem.

Light and heat from the Sun . . .   *. . . helps the grass grow.*

Zebras feed on the grass . . .   *. . . and provide food for lions.*

THE ECOSYSTEM JIGSAW

An ecosystem is like a jigsaw puzzle. It is made up of living things, such as plants and animals, and nonliving things, such as water and the Sun's energy.

All the pieces in the ecosystem jigsaw must fit together. If there's not enough rain on the African savanna, the grass withers and dies. Then the zebras that feed on the grass die, too. So do the lions that feed on the zebras.

All ecosystems, big and small, work in this way. A healthy ecosystem has many different species living in it. Each species helps keep the ecosystem working.

In a well-balanced ocean ecosystem, sea otters and kelp help each other survive.

PESKY RABBITS

Humans often bring new plants or animals to an ecosystem. This can upset the delicate balance in that system. In 1859, in Australia, Thomas Austin released 24 rabbits into his farm. With no foxes around to hunt them, the rabbit population exploded. There are now 200-300 million rabbits in Australia! They eat so many plants that many native animals find it hard to survive.

A TEAM EFFORT

If one group of animals or plants disappears from an ecosystem, the whole ecosystem can break down. For example, sea otters might leave an area of the ocean. Then the sea urchins they feed on will multiply. The urchins will then eat so much kelp that the remaining kelp forest will die. With no kelp forest where sea otters can hide from sharks, killer whales, and other large predators, the sea otters will not return to the area.

Nature has its own way of keeping balance. If a community gets too big, it is often reduced by lack of food or by predators, drought, disease, or fire (below).

YOUR ECOSYSTEM AND YOU

Keep an ecosystem journal in a notebook for one week.

1) Write down as many ecosystems as you can spot around you. Keep in mind that an ecosystem might be as large as your backyard or as small as a single tree, or the patch of soil beneath a rock!

2) Write down as many living factors as you can spot, such as specific types of plants and animals. Also write down the nonliving factors that you can spot, such as soil, or a pond (water source) or a rubbish bin (potential food source for wild animals).

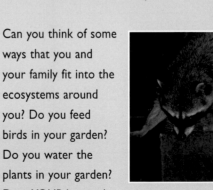

3) Can you think of some ways that you and your family fit into the ecosystems around you? Do you feed birds in your garden? Do you water the plants in your garden? Does YOUR home also provide a home for birds or insects?

How do the different members of the ecosystems around you depend on one another. How do they help each other?

CHAPTER 2:
How It All Works

All living things need energy to grow, move around, and reproduce. Luckily, on Earth we have a constant source of energy – the Sun. Without it, life as we know it could not exist. Green plants use the Sun's energy to make their own food. This process is known as photosynthesis. Through photosynthesis, plants use energy from sunlight to convert water and carbon dioxide into food. This process also produces the oxygen that humans and animals need to breathe to stay alive.

THE ENERGY CHAIN

Animals can't produce their own food. Some animals get their energy from eating plants. Other animals get their energy by chomping on animals that have eaten plants. But the energy chain doesn't stop there. Plants and animals release waste throughout their lives. This waste, which may be in the form of food or gases, returns energy back into the environment. And when plants and animals die, their remains rot, or decompose, and add nutrition to the soil.

Plants use sunlight to turn air and water into sugars. These sugars can then be used by the plants – and the animals that eat them – as food. This giraffe gets its energy from leaves high in the treetops.

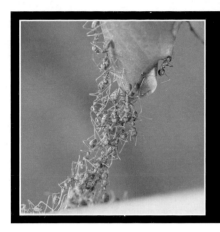

BIG BIOMASS!

The combined weight of a species or type of organism is called its biomass. In the animal world, humans seem the dominant species. But we make up less than 0.5% of all animal biomass. All the ants in the world probably weigh at least twenty times more than all the humans!

TOP OF THE HEAP

An ecological pyramid illustrates how energy is passed on as it moves up the food chain of animals in an ecosystem. As energy flows through an ecosystem, some of it gets lost on the way. For example, animals lose heat from their bodies. Since there is less energy further up the food chain, there are also fewer animals near the top of the chain.

AN ORCA'S ECOLOGICAL PYRAMID

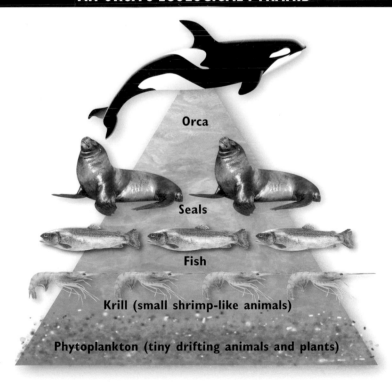

Orca

Seals

Fish

Krill (small shrimp-like animals)

Phytoplankton (tiny drifting animals and plants)

Orcas (killer whales) are at the top of their food chain. They are much bigger than fish and other organisms lower down. In terms of biomass, however, the combined weight of all the organisms the orcas eat is greater than the weight of all the orcas.

ENERGY FROM THE SUN TO YOUR TABLE

1) These corn plants use light from the Sun to turn air and water into sugars. The sugars can then be used by the plant as food. The energy in the sugars is passed on to the animals that eat the plant.

2) A field of corn uses energy from the Sun to produce the nourishment it needs to grow. When it is ripe, the corn is harvested and the ears of corn are separated from their stalks.

3) Corn that is grown for animals to eat is loaded into silos or other feeding bins. Ears of corn produced for humans to eat are displayed and sold in food markets.

4) A plateful of steaming-hot corn provides energy, flavour, and fun when prepared as nature provided it – right on the cob!

Elephants must take in huge quantities of water to carry nutrition to every part of their large bodies. This is why they spend a great deal of their time near water supplies.

NATURAL CYCLES

Ecosystems are not just about animals eating each other and passing on energy. Plants and animals also need water, carbon, nitrogen, and other important elements to help them grow and repair their bodies. These elements are recycled again and again.

WATER

Water is a key part of life. You could survive for many weeks without food, but you would only last a few days without water. Water carries nutrients around inside all organisms. It also helps remove waste. That's why there is so much water in our bodies (and those of most animals). About 70 percent of an adult human's body is made up of water!

The water on our planet is constantly going through a huge recycling process called the water cycle. The water cycle moves water from the oceans up into the atmosphere, down to the land and back again.

THE CARBON CYCLE

Carbon is an element that is found in every living thing. It is found in many nonliving things, too. Plants absorb carbon dioxide from the atmosphere during photosynthesis. They then use the carbon to make carbohydrates. When animals eat plants, this carbon is passed on. Humans and animals give out carbon as carbon dioxide gas. They put carbon into the atmosphere every time they breathe out.

Animals are living stores of carbon. When they die, their rotting bodies return most of this carbon back to the atmosphere. All dead plants and animals contribute important nutrients and other substances to the soil when they die.

THE WATER CYCLE

2. The warm water vapour (gas) rises in the air, where it cools and forms tiny droplets. This is called condensation. The droplets mass together to form clouds.

3. As the drops get heavier, they fall as rain or snow. This is called precipitation.

4. Rivers carry the rainwater back to the sea. The process of water gathering on Earth is called accumulation.

1. The Sun warms the sea's surface, causing the water to turn into vapour. This is called evaporation.

The water on our planet gets used over and over again. The raindrops falling on your head contain the same water that fell on the dinosaurs over 65 million years ago.

THE ULTIMATE BIRTHDAY GIFT!

Salmon give their young an amazing birthday present – their own dead bodies! Soon after adult salmon spawn (lay their eggs), they die. Their rotting bodies add nutrients to the water. This is one way that young salmon get nourishment from the water. But some youngsters go right to the source – the dead bodies of their parents!

MAKE YOUR OWN WATER CYCLE

Materials needed
- A large plastic bowl
- A jug of water
- An elastic band
- A small plastic container
- Some clingfilm

1) Place a small container in the centre of a large plastic bowl.

2) Pour some water into the small container.

3) Stretch a sheet of clingfilm over the bowl and fasten it snugly with a piece of string or a large elastic band.

4) Place the bowl in the Sun.

The Sun will heat the water and cause it to evaporate, or turn into water vapour. The vapour will rise into the 'atmosphere' above the water in the bowl. If the plastic sheet is not too warm, the vapour will cool when it touches the plastic. It will then turn back into water droplets. These droplets will fall, like 'rain' into the bowl. You have created a miniature water cycle!

Without dung, our world would be a less pleasant place in which to live! We would have less nitrogen in the atmosphere and would have to use more artificial fertiliser on our crops.

MINERAL CYCLES – THE NITROGEN CYCLE

Decomposing dung (manure) isn't everyone's favourite sight (or smell). But it is part of another important cycle – the nitrogen cycle. Nitrogen is a gas. It makes up 78 percent of Earth's atmosphere. All living things need nitrogen to build protein.

Plants and animals can't process this gas, but they can soak up nitrates in the ground. Nitrates contain nitrogen. They are created by bacteria, lichens, and algae. Nitrates help plants grow. When cows eat grass, they consume nitrates. And when they deposit dung, they also deposit nitrates. That is why the grass around rotting cow manure is often greener. Dung flies get into the act, too. When these flies eat manure, they stir up small particles of the manure. This motion helps release the nitrates consumed by the animal.

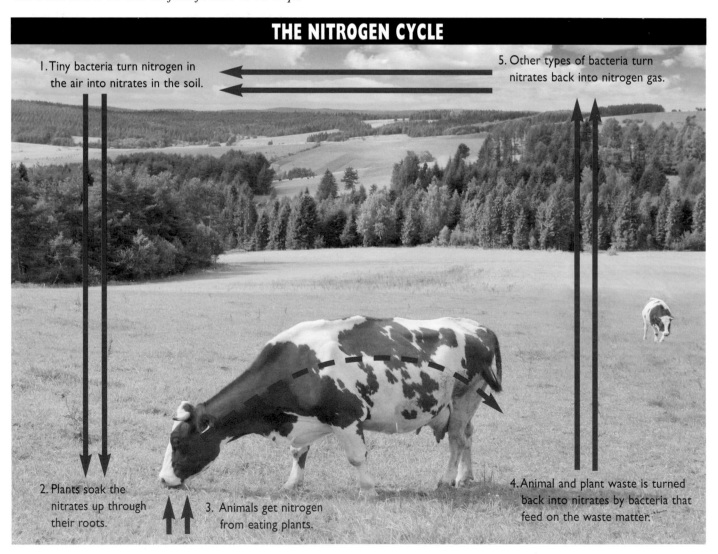

THE NITROGEN CYCLE

1. Tiny bacteria turn nitrogen in the air into nitrates in the soil.

5. Other types of bacteria turn nitrates back into nitrogen gas.

2. Plants soak the nitrates up through their roots.

3. Animals get nitrogen from eating plants.

4. Animal and plant waste is turned back into nitrates by bacteria that feed on the waste matter.

Too many man-made artificial nitrates in the soil can get into our drinking water and the atmosphere. Scientists suspect that taking in too many nitrates may cause diseases such as cancer or asthma.

TOO MUCH OF A GOOD THING

Farmers use nitrates as fertilisers to grow more crops. But the need for more nitrates has grown. Today we have developed ways of making artificial nitrates. But these artificial nitrates overload the natural system. As a result, they may hurt the ecological balance. Too many nitrates in rivers and lakes help algae grow in large numbers. The algae then use up oxygen in the water, killing fish and other wildlife.

OTHER MINERALS

Other important minerals are used by animals and plants. They include phosphorus, iron, sulphur, and calcium. Many of these minerals form in rocks deep underground. Most of them are then brought to the surface by volcanoes. On land, most animals get minerals from the water they drink. In the sea, shellfish take calcium from the water. The shellfish use the calcium to make their shells.

THE MINERAL CYCLE

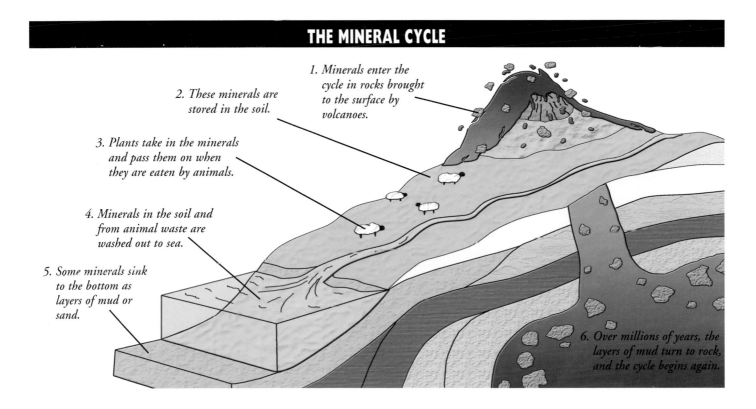

1. Minerals enter the cycle in rocks brought to the surface by volcanoes.

2. These minerals are stored in the soil.

3. Plants take in the minerals and pass them on when they are eaten by animals.

4. Minerals in the soil and from animal waste are washed out to sea.

5. Some minerals sink to the bottom as layers of mud or sand.

6. Over millions of years, the layers of mud turn to rock, and the cycle begins again.

Sharks and other tertiary consumers get lots of energy from eating meat. They need it. It's much harder work catching a seal than waiting for prey to simply drop by!

CHAPTER 3:
Living In An Ecosystem

The living things in an ecosystem are linked together by food chains. Food chains show who eats what, or whom!

Most often, at the bottom of the chain are plants, known as producers. They use the Sun's energy to make their own nutrition. This nutrition is passed on to plant-eating animals, known as primary consumers. They in turn are eaten by secondary consumers – meat-eaters. At the top of the chain are big predators, such as lions and sharks – the tertiary consumers.

A food web combines food chains. These food chains interact with one another. Members of the same food web may compete with one another for food.

FOOD WEBS AND INTERDEPENDENCE

In this diagram, the arrows point in the direction in which energy travels up a food chain. It also shows interdependence between species. For example, the number of insects in a garden depends on how many birds eat the insects. It also depends on how many plants there are for the insects to eat.

IT'S A DIRTY JOB, BUT SOMEBODY'S GOT TO DO IT!

An elephant munches away all day, but much of what it eats goes straight through it! So why is the ground not permanently covered with elephant droppings? Animals and plants known as decomposers feed off droppings. Decomposers break down the waste of other living things. Bacteria and fungi do most of the hard work. They are helped by maggots (usually fly larvae), dung beetles, and earthworms. Decomposers speed up the process of decomposition. In this way, they help put minerals back into the soil.

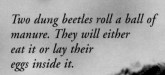

Two dung beetles roll a ball of manure. They will either eat it or lay their eggs inside it.

PREDATORS AND THEIR PREY

Every ecosystem has its share of interesting characters in its community of predators and prey.

CHEETAHS

Cheetahs can run at over 100 kilometres per hour. However, the chase leaves them very worn out. They often have to rest for twenty minutes before they eat their kill.

A PREDATOR PLANT

The Venus flytrap has short, stiff trigger hairs on its leaves. When an insect touches a trigger hair, the leaf snaps shut and traps the insect. Inside, the plant has digestive juices to dissolve the insect's soft parts. After a few days, the leaf opens up again. The leftover hard pieces of the insect blow away.

SCAVENGER'S DELIGHT

Scavengers are animals such as flies, wasps, ravens, cockroaches, and even raccoons that eat dead animals and break them into little pieces. In this way, scavengers help start the process of decomposition. Vultures are among the best known scavengers. Here a vulture has begun tearing apart the body of a dead cow.

DON'T GO NEAR THE WATER!

Piranhas live in rainforest rivers in South America. They change their behaviour with the seasons. During the wet season, they are usually scavengers. But in the dry season, piranhas can turn into hunters. As the river water levels go down, big groups of piranhas are forced to cluster in small patches of water. Together, they will attack large animals, that come to the river to drink. A piranha group can strip all the flesh off a large animal in just a few minutes!

WHAT MAKES A PERFECT HOME?

Animals living in an ecosystem are affected by the other animals and plants around them. But their environment also has a big impact on them. For desert plants and animals finding and storing water is a much bigger problem than it is for animals that live in a rain forest. This is one reason that fewer plants and animals live in a desert than in a rainforest.

Almost all ecosystems depend on the Sun. The Sun provides energy for plants to make food. It also drives the water cycle by evaporating water into the atmosphere.

BIOTIC OR ABIOTIC

An ecosystem is affected by both living and nonliving factors. Soil, rocks, sunlight, and weather are all nonliving. They are known as abiotic factors. Animals and plants are living, or biotic factors. Many animals and plants can only survive if the abiotic factors are just right. For example, the larvae (young) of spotted salamanders can only survive in water. Adult salamanders live on land. However, they must be near water in order to breed and lay their eggs.

Some animals have adapted to extreme abiotic factors. Teleost fish live in icy polar waters. Their bodies make a natural chemical that keeps their blood from freezing.

ABIOTIC FACTORS

LIGHT AND HEAT
The Sun provides the energy plants need to make food. The Sun's energy also keeps animals warm.

LACK OF SUNLIGHT
In a shady wooded area, some grasses and other plants don't get enough sunlight for photosynthesis.

WATER
Without water there would be no life.

Look at this picture of Monument Valley, Arizona, USA. What abiotic factors can you see here? Compare the abiotic factors in this ecosystem with the abiotic factors where you live.

PLANTS AND ABIOTIC FACTORS

Materials needed
- Mung bean seeds
- 4 plastic plant pots
- Potting compost
- Watering can

1) Fill each plant pot with potting compost. Plant a mung bean in each pot just below the surface of the soil. Label the pots A, B, C, and D.

2) Place pots A and B in a bright, sunny spot. Then put pots C and D in a dark corner.

3) Now water only pots A and C every day.

Which plant do you think will grow the best? It should be plant A, as it is getting both light and water. Plant C isn't getting enough light, and plant B isn't getting water. Without light or water, plant D may not grow at all!

SOIL
Soil provides important nutrients that help plants grow. It also holds water for plants and animals to use.

ATMOSPHERE
Our atmosphere is the giant blanket of air around the Earth. It provides oxygen and carbon dioxide to the ecosystem.

SHELTER
Cracks in a rock or an old wall provide shelter for snails, ants, wasps, and other tiny creatures.

SURVIVAL

Every ecosystem, whether it is big or small, is affected by abiotic factors. Many plants thrive in sunlight. Others do better in a cool, shady area beneath a tree. Plants have a better chance of surviving if they need different abiotic factors to survive. This way, there are plenty of resources to go around.

Predators and abiotic factors ensure that no one plant or animal takes over. What if a small swarm of fruit flies had no predators and an endless supply of food? In less than a year there would be enough fruit flies to cover the entire planet! In nature, the numbers are kept down by the lack of food, lots of hungry predators, extreme weather, and disease.

POPULATIONS

All the animals in one species that live in an ecosystem are called a population. As populations get bigger or smaller, their effect on the rest of the ecosystem changes. All of the different populations in an ecosystem make up the community of that ecosystem.

Moss, like that growing on the side of this tree, survives when the abiotic factors in its environment include dampness and shade from sunlight.

NICHES

A niche describes the role that a plant or animal plays in its environment. An animal's niche also tells us something about what it does, how it behaves, and the way it uses what is around it to survive. Niches also help animals and plants avoid competition for the same resources.

Unlike other species in their ecosystem, pandas feed almost entirely on bamboo. Feeding on a plant that almost no other animal eats helps pandas survive. This type of feeding creates a special niche for pandas in their ecosystem.

WINTER BREAK

Many animals' bodies have adapted over millions of years. These adaptations might help the animal find food, hide from predators, or survive in its habitat. During the winter, when food is scarce, bears go into a state resembling sleep. This state is called hibernation. While a bear is hibernating, its body uses up less energy and can live off its stored fat.

GETTING ALONG

Animals and plants living together in the same ecosystem make space for themselves in different ways:

SPREADING OUT

In a tropical rainforest, animals avoid competing with each other by living at different levels. Birds live in treetops. Monkeys live in branches. Leopards and other larger animals spend most of their time on the forest floor.

KEEPING A LOOKOUT

Many animals, such as flocks of birds or herds of deer, live in groups. This allows some animals to keep a lookout for danger while others are eating. Lions and wolves hunt in groups so they can bring down buffalo, moose, and other large prey.

MARKING TERRITORY

Tigers are big hunters. They eat so much that they cannot afford to compete with other tigers in the same patch of forest. They urinate and leave scratch marks on trees to tell other tigers to 'keep out.'

CHAPTER 4:
Biomes

The world is divided into large regions called biomes. Every place on Earth is part of a biome. Most biomes support a wide variety of plant and animal life. Others, such as the polar regions of Antarctica and the Arctic, are so extreme that a limited number of species have adapted to life there.

Central American rainforests are a perfect home for the glasswing butterfly. It receives nutrition from nectar in the tropical plants it visits.

The Arctic provides polar bears with plenty of seals and fish for their diet. Humans that live in the bears' habitat also provide a source of food – rubbish!

LIFE ON LAND

Let's take a walking tour of some of Earth's biomes. We'll start at the Equator and head north.

When you stand at the Equator, you're probably in a rainforest biome. **Tropical rainforests** are hot and very rainy for much of the year. If you walk north, where it is still hot but rains less, you would come across the subtropical forests of India or the dry **savanna** of East Africa. You might even find yourself in the subtropical wetlands of southern Florida known as the Everglades! Keep going!

Further north, you come across hot, dry **deserts** in Africa, Asia, or North America. **Temperate grasslands** and **deciduous forests** await you in Europe, North America, and Asia. These biomes have warm summers and cold winters.

As you get closer to the North Pole, the trees are more likely to be conifers, part of the great northern **conifer forests** that stretch across Asia and North America. Finally you will reach the cold deserts of the **tundra** and the icy **Arctic** regions of the far north.

EARTH'S BIOMES

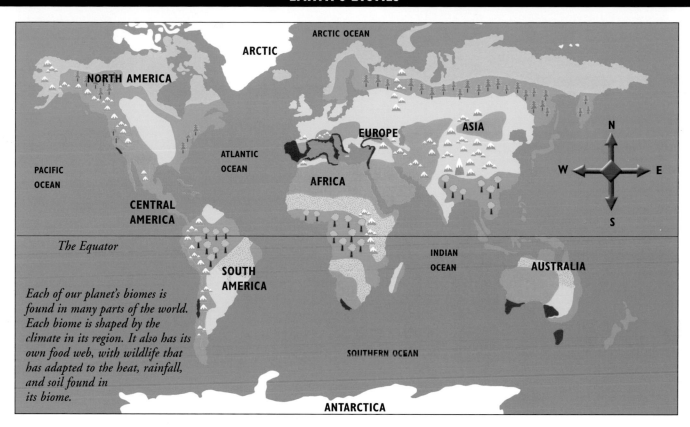

The Equator

Each of our planet's biomes is found in many parts of the world. Each biome is shaped by the climate in its region. It also has its own food web, with wildlife that has adapted to the heat, rainfall, and soil found in its biome.

TEMPERATE GRASSLANDS
Warm and dry summers, cool or cold winters; enough rainfall to support a variety of animal life

SAVANNA
Large plains with scattered trees and bushes; usually hot all year round

DESERT
Dry land, little rain; few plants other than cacti, which store water in their stems

TUNDRA
Cold, windy desert-like plains, mostly in Siberia; land frozen just below surface

ARCTIC/ANTARCTICA
Extremely cold and dry all year; frozen ground and icy seas; no plant life

OCEANS
Warm and cold seas supporting animals from microscopic plankton to vast mammals

CHAPARRAL
Flat plains, rocky hills, mountain slopes; plants and animals adapted to hot, dry summers, mild winters

TEMPERATE DECIDUOUS FOREST
Vegetation that blooms and thrives in summer, usually dormant in winter

CONIFEROUS FOREST
Cold evergreen forest; most animals migrate or hibernate in winter

TROPICAL RAINFOREST
Hot, wet climate, with lots of sun and rain supporting huge variety of life

ISLAND WONDERS

Islands often have unique ecosystems. Lemurs are only found on Madagascar. The marine iguana (pictured here) and giant tortoises only live on the Galápagos Islands in the Pacific Ocean. The marine iguana is the only sea-going lizard in the world. It dives in the sea to find seaweed to eat.

THE BLUE PLANET

Earth is often called the Blue Planet. This photograph from space shows why. About 70 percent of Earth's surface is covered by water.

LIFE IN THE WATER

The oceans make up the largest biome on our planet. The food webs here contain everything from giant whales to microscopic phytoplankton.

The ocean needs the Sun to give its animal and plant communities food and energy. Microscopic organisms called phytoplankton help with this process. Billions of phytoplankton float near the surface of the ocean. Here they use light from the Sun to make food for themselves. Then, they become food for bigger animals. Through the ocean food web, the Sun's energy is passed on up, even to humans if we eat fish!

AN INLAND SEA

Lake Baikal is a freshwater sea in Siberia. It is frozen for more than five months a year. But underneath the ice there is a remarkable ecosystem. Part of the lake's community are the nerpa. These freshwater seals can hold their breath for over 70 minutes. In spring, tourists come to Lake Baikal for fishing holidays. They catch the many species of fish that live just below the lake's icy surface.

Compared to salt water, fresh water is rare on our planet. Just 0.3 percent of Earth's fresh water flows as rivers or sits in lakes. Most of the planet's fresh water is frozen as ice at the poles and in glaciers. However, ponds, rivers, and lakes all contain rich freshwater ecosystems. Their communities often use energy and food created by producers on land, such as fallen leaves.

With thousands of different species living together in a small area, coral reefs are complete ecosystems. The corals are groups of tiny animals. These animals create limestone shells. Within the coral animals are tiny single-celled algae. The algae use energy from the Sun to produce food for the coral. The coral then releases nutrients to other types of algae. In this way, these members of the ecosystem help one another survive.

WATER ECOSYSTEMS

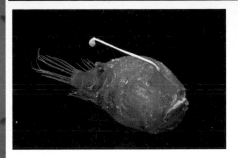

THE OCEANS
The ocean biome contains many ecosystems. In the deepest parts of the Earth's oceans ecosystems have developed where animals are adapted to life in the dark. The angler fish swims around with a lighted, fleshy 'fishing rod' on its head. When the light attracts other fish, the angler fish quickly snaps them up.

RIVERS
Five thousand species of fish live in the Amazon River, in South America. One inhabitant of this river ecosystem is the electric eel. It can stun its prey with a 600-volt electric shock. Other members of the Amazon community are predators such as freshwater dolphins, otters, turtles, and giant anaconda snakes.

EXTREME BIOMES

There are ecosystems everywhere on Earth, even in the most extreme biomes. In Antarctica, for example, Emperor penguins live with temperatures and wind that would freeze exposed human flesh in seconds.

At the other extreme is the baking heat of a sandy desert. In desert biomes, plants such as cacti can survive years of drought on water collected from a single rainfall. Animals such as kangaroo rats, snakes, and lizards are busy at night to avoid the daytime heat. During the day, they lie in burrows or under rocks.

Mountains are home to a wide range of plants and animals that can survive temperatures that go from baking to freezing in just a few hours. As you climb up a mountain, the climate, soil, and plant life change over very short distances.

LIFE AT INCREDIBLE DEPTHS

At least one and a half kilometres beneath the ocean surface, deep-sea vents gush out hot water loaded with minerals. Bacteria use the heat and minerals to make food. These bacteria and the food they produce are part of a food web that includes the tubeworm (below). The tubeworm exists on the food created by the bacteria. Tubeworms form protective tubes around themselves using their own secretions. The tubes can grow as long as six metres.

The cardon cactus lives in the Sonoran Desert, which is in the USA and Mexico. It is the largest cactus in the world. The cardon's trunk can store almost a tonne of water at one time. Its branches point up. This reduces how much of its surface faces the full effects of the hot Sun.

SURVIVING EXTREME CONDITIONS

SPADE-FOOT TOAD

The spade-foot toad lives in hot deserts in the southwest of the USA. It avoids the heat by hibernating underground for most of the year.

BACTRIAN CAMEL

The Gobi Desert in central Asia combines freezing cold winters with short, baking summers. The Bactrian camel can survive both. In winter, it grows a thick coat and gets water from drinking snow. In summer, it can go for months without water.

EMPEROR PENGUINS

Emperor penguins mate and lay eggs in the winter when Antarctic temperatures are as low as − 40°C. For over two months, each father bird stands in freezing conditions incubating the egg on his feet. This enables the chick to hatch in spring, and gives it the best chance of survival.

The Saskatchewan Glacier, in Banff National Park, Canada. The glacier is retreating.

It has not yet fully retreated, but where it has, plant life is taking hold.

Aldabra, a coral island in the Indian Ocean, has come a long way. Today it is an ecosystem with many animal and plant species – and, according to a recent count, 10–20 human inhabitants!

CHAPTER 5: Changing Ecosystems

When left to themselves, farmers' fields and gardens alike soon become covered with weeds. Taller plants arrive and choke the grass, and different species take over as the ecosystem develops. The order in which new life comes into a habitat and joins an ecosystem is called succession.

RECLAIMING A HABITAT

A lot of forest land that is now filled with plants and animals was buried under glaciers for centuries. The glaciers have now retreated slowly back to the Arctic. After a glacier has retreated, it usually takes hundreds of years for the land to be fully reclaimed by nature.

THE BIRTH OF AN ISLAND

Above water, the rough surface of a coral reef is not an ideal place for plants and animals to live on. But over time, the reef's limestone shell is worn away by wind and rain. The rock breaks into small grains that become soil. Over time, seeds blow onto the reef and settle in the soil. They grow into plants. As these plants die, their waste makes the soil even richer. This allows

FOREST FIRES: A NEW BEGINNING?

Many plants and animals have adapted to fire. As shown here (right), fires do not necessarily mean the end of forest ecosystems. The heat of a forest fire may cause the cones of a jack pine to burst open, scattering thousands of seeds to the ground. New grasses from beneath the charred forest floor may poke their way through. And woodpeckers and other birds may return to feed on beetles and other insects that have moved into burned-out trees.

larger plants to grow and provides food and shelter for animals. In time, what was once an uninviting habitat can become a lush, fertile tropical island!

Just about any surface will give way to a habitat's original plant life if left alone for long enough!

NEW SPECIES IN YOUR BACKYARD

Materials needed
• Large container, such as an empty fish tank
• Sample of pond water
• Magnifying lens

1) Collect a sample of pond or rain water and put it in a large glass container, such as an empty fish tank. Leave it in direct sunlight.

2) After a day, take a look at the glass. You will probably see that algae are quick to move in!

3) Check the water every few days with a simple magnifier. You may also spot other small animals in the water. For an even better look, examine samples of water in a shallow dish.

4) If you'd like new life to come more quickly, add small pieces of dried grass or hay and other plant material to the container to speed things up!

This experiment shows how new species might appear in a new habitat. Often the first to arrive are algae, microscopic organisms that drift around in the air until they find a pond or damp place to live in.

WHAT CAN WE DO?

MAKING ROOM FOR WILDLIFE
Cities are ecosystems, too. Areas of wasteland can be turned into wildlife meadows. Garden ponds and trees provide food and shelter for many smaller animals.

PLEASE TAKE
NOTHING BUT
PICTURES
LEAVE NOTHING
BUT FOOTPRINTS

WATER = LIFE
As Earth's human population grows, we are running out of fresh water. But today many people are battling to conserve wetlands, rivers, and lakes. They want to attract animals and other wildlife back to their original habitats.

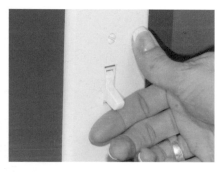

GETTING EVERYONE INVOLVED
You can get involved! You can turn off lights when you are not using them. Or you can reduce the heating by a couple of degrees. Every time you do these things, you reduce your need for energy resources and help the environment.

HUMANS AND ECOSYSTEMS

In the last two hundred years, humans have had a huge impact on ecosystems all over the planet. Today, Earth's ecosystems are more threatened than at any other time in human history. The tropical rainforest, for example, is being cut down to clear space for farming. This activity destroys animal and plant habitats. Some of the plants in rainforests may have uses as medicines or foods, but we will never know if they are destroyed.

Burning fossil fuels has polluted the atmosphere. Modern farming has removed woodlands. Weed killers and insecticides poison both the soil and wildlife species. Decomposers cannot break down plastics and other products made by humans.

The speed of these changes gives individual species little or no time to adapt. Today, in fact, species are being wiped out faster than at any other time in the past 10,000 years. We need to find new ways of living and creating energy that leave ecosystems in balance.

Healthy ecosystems are good for all living things. They provide us with the food we eat. They also provide us with clean air and water. And perhaps even more importantly, they assure the survival of an ecologically balanced planet for generations to come.

The growth of towns, cities, and farmland can divide wildlife communities. Today, there are two surviving populations of mountain gorillas in Africa. These two groups are based in two separate areas of national park. These two areas are 45 kilometres apart from each other.

Landfill sites – the next ecosystem? It's hard to imagine. But with areas the size of this landfill, it may only be a matter of time before a variety of organisms move in. And few of them are likely to be ones that we would welcome with open arms!

TOO HIGH A PRICE FOR SUCCESS?

The Alaska pipeline in the USA helps transport oil across vast distances. But many feel that it is unsightly against the beauty of a natural landscape. Even more important is the effect it has on wildlife. The pipeline has disturbed the migration routes of herds of reindeer. In turn, this affects wolves and other predators who depend on the migrating reindeer for food.

GLOSSARY

abiotic factors The nonliving parts of an ecosystem, such as water, sunlight, soil, climate, or rocks.

algae Microscopic organisms that make their own energy using photosynthesis, like plants. They drift around in the air until they find a pond or damp place to live in.

adaptation The process by which a plant or animal changes over time to suit its surroundings. An animal's body may change physically, or the animal may change its behaviour.

atmosphere The thick layer of air that surrounds the Earth. The gases that make up Earth's atmosphere include nitrogen (78%) and oxygen (21%). There is also water, and small quantities of other gases such as argon, greenhouse gases and carbon dioxide.

bacteria A kind of single-celled organism which can only be seen through a microscope. Some bacteria cause diseases.

biomass The total weight of living organisms, either plants or animals.

biome A large region with similar climate, weather, and plant and animal life. Examples of biomes include rainforest, ocean and desert.

biotic factors The living parts of an ecosystem, such as plants and animals.

carbohydrates The sugars and starches found in many foods. They are made up of carbon, hydrogen, and oxygen.

climate The average weather in an area over a long period of time.

condensation The process by which a gas such as water vapour changes into a liquid.

decompose To decay or rot.

dung Animal droppings.

ecological pyramid A way of showing how energy is lost as you go up the food chain. There may be millions of animals or plants at the bottom of the chain, but far fewer animals or plants can live at the top.

ecosystem A natural system made up of a community of plants and animals. Many ecosystems can exist within one habitat. The study of ecosystems is called ecology. The scientists who study ecology are called ecologists.

environment The objects and conditions, such as climate, soil, and living things, that surround and act upon a habitat. These things also affect the ecosystems that are part of that habitat.

evaporation The process by which a liquid (such as water) turns into a gas (such as water vapour).

fertiliser A substance used by farmers to make soil more fertile, so that more plants can grow.

food chain The relationship between plants and animals that shows who eats what and who.

food web A set of linked food chains that shows who eats what and who in an ecosystem.

fossil fuel Oil, natural gas and coal. They are called fossil fuels because they were made from the decaying remains of animals, plants and other organisms.

fresh water Water that is not salty, and which can be used by humans, animals, and plants. The water in ponds, lakes, rivers and streams is usually fresh water.

fungi A group of organisms such as mushrooms, moulds, yeast, and mildew.

glacier A huge, slow-moving river of ice (usually around 30 metres thick). The glacier moves slowly down a slope or valley. Some glaciers move only a few centimetres a year. Others travel up to one metre a day.

habitat A specific area, small or large, that is home to a plant or animal and provides all that animal or plant's needs.

interdependence The process by which living things depend on one another for survival.

kelp forest An underwater forest of tall, brown seaweed. Kelp is a type of algae.

krill Shrimplike creatures found in huge numbers in open seas. Krill is the main food source for many large marine animals, particularly baleen whales.

landfill site A huge hole in the ground where many tons of rubbish are buried. Eventually the rubbish is covered over with soil.

larvae The young of insects and amphibians. Larvae hatch from eggs. They often look very different from adults. For example, tadpoles are the larvae of frogs.

lichens Plants that are a combination of a fungus and an algae.

minerals Solid, inorganic substances that occur naturally on Earth, such as copper, iron and salt. Some minerals are used by plants and animals.

mineral cycle The movement of minerals from deep inside Earth, into soil, the oceans, plants and animals. Eventually the minerals return to Earth again.

niche A unique role in an ecosystem. The niche of a bee, for example, is to pollinate flowers. By performing this role, the bee helps the plant to reproduce.

nutrients The minerals and substances that plants and animals need to grow and develop.

organism A living thing.

photosynthesis How plants convert carbon dioxide and water into food (carbohydrates) by using the energy in sunlight.

phytoplankton Microscopic floating plants.

pollute To contaminate or make impure or unclean. For example, fertilisers used on farms can contaminate water, making it poisonous and killing plants and animals.

precipitation Any form of water (for example, rain or snow) that falls to Earth's surface.

predator An animal that lives by killing and eating other animals.

prey An animal that is hunted or eaten for food by another animal.

scavenger An animal that feeds on the bodies of animals that are already dead.

sea urchins Sea animals with bodies covered with spines.

spawn To produce or fertilise eggs.

succession The order in which plants and animals colonise a habitat.

water cycle The constant movement of water from rivers, lakes, and the ocean up into the atmosphere and back down to Earth.